★ *GREAT SPORTS TEAMS* ★

THE NOTRE DAME

FIGHTING
IRISH

FOOTBALL TEAM

David Aretha

Enslow Publishers, Inc.

40 Industrial Road   PO Box 38
Box 398   Aldershot
Berkeley Heights, NJ 07922   Hants GU12 6BP
USA   UK

http://www.enslow.com

Library of Congress Cataloging-in-Publication Data

Aretha, David.
    The Notre Dame Fighting Irish football team / David Aretha.
        p. cm. — (Great sports teams)
    Includes bibliographical references and index.
    ISBN 0-7660-1486-X
      1. Notre Dame Fighting Irish (Football team)—History—Juvenile literature.
    [1. Notre Dame Fighting Irish (Football team)—History. 2. Football—History.]
    I. Title. II. Series.
    GV958.U54 A74   2001
    796.332′63′0977289—dc21

                                  00-012216

Printed in the United States of America

10 9 8 7 6 5 4 3 2 1

To Our Readers: We have done our best to make sure all Internet addresses in this book were active and appropriate when we went to press. However, the author and the publisher have no control over and assume no liability for the material available on those Internet sites or on other Web sites they may link to. Any comments or suggestions can be sent by e-mail to comments@enslow.com or to the address on the back cover.

CONTENTS

1 The Gipper 5

2 Team History 11

3 The Legends 17

4 The Men in Charge 23

5 Dream Seasons 29

6 Today 35

Statistics 40

Chapter Notes 43

Glossary 45

Further Reading 46

Index 47

Where to Write and Internet Sites 48

George Gipp is shown here in a rare photo from 1915. Gipp played for the Notre Dame football team from 1917 to 1920.

THE GIPPER

otre Dame's George Gipp, the most dynamic player in college football, lay in a bed at St. Joseph's Hospital. Head Coach Knute Rockne could see how sad the Gipper had become. He looked frail and gaunt, his voice reduced to a whisper. He was dying from a combination of pneumonia and strep throat.

Three weeks earlier, Gipp had thrown for 157 yards on six passes as the Fighting Irish fans chanted, "Gipp, Gipp, Gipp!" Days later, Gipp began to weaken. He was tired and faint and he had a terrible cough. He was taken to the hospital, but his condition worsened. As news spread across campus, students prayed for their beloved hero. Gipp, however, knew he would never leave that hospital bed.

"Rock," he whispered to his coach, "I know I'm going to die. I'm not afraid. But someday, Rock, when things on the field are going against us, tell the boys,

Rock, to go out and win just one for the Gipper. Now, I don't know where I'll be then, Coach. But I'll know about it, and I'll be happy."[1]

Rockne, tears welling, placed his hand on Gipp's forehead. "Rock, one more thing, please," Gipp said. "I'd like to see a priest."[2]

Rockne had first seen Gipp playing on a practice field in early September 1916. Rockne was awestruck by the gangly lad's 60-yard drop-kick. Gipp joined the varsity in 1917 and became an All-American in 1920. He could pass, catch, kick 50-yard field goals, and run all day. Defensively, he never allowed a single pass to be completed in his zone in his entire college career. The Irish fans fell in love with him, though he remained a quiet hero.

"He was a loner," said Rockne. "Seemed to live for the moment."[3]

An Immortal Player

Gipp's greatest moment came against Army on October 30, 1920. Infuriated by Army's dirty play, Gipp became a one-man show. He passed, ran, caught, and returned to the tune of 480 total yards. In the fourth quarter, he returned a kick 50 yards to secure a 27–17 Irish triumph.

As one newspaper reported: "George Gipp galloped wild through the Army on the plains here this afternoon, giving a performance which was more like an antelope's than a human being's."[4]

Notre Dame fans carried Gipp off the field that day. Six weeks later, they marched with him again,

*T*he Gipper was one of the most versatile football players in Notre Dame's history. He could run, pass, catch, and kick, as well as play defense.

only this time after a memorial service at St. Mary's Cathedral. Despite a fierce snowstorm, the Notre Dame student body escorted the casket on a solemn walk through campus.

The Gipper was gone, but his legend would live on forever.

"One for the Gipper"

Eight years later, in 1928, Rockne's boys were struggling through a 4–2 season. On November 10, they faced Army. Army was undefeated at the time and considered the best team in the country. In front of almost seventy-eight thousand fans in New York's Yankee Stadium, the two teams battled through a hard-hitting, scoreless first half.

During halftime, Rockne cleared virtually all non–team members out of the locker room. Somber and speaking in a hushed voice, he told the story of the Gipper. He concluded: "You know, boys, just before he died, George Gipp called me over. And in phrases that were barely whispers, he said, 'Someday, Rock, when things on the field are going against us, tell the boys, Rock, to go out and win just one for the Gipper. Now, I don't know where I'll be then, Coach. But I'll know about it, and I'll be happy.'"[5]

Coaches and players could not hold back their tears. Flooded with emotion, the Fighting Irish charged out of the locker room.

Army took a 6–0 lead before Notre Dame's Jack Chevigny busted in for a touchdown. "That's one for the Gipper," he said. "Let's get another."[6]

The Notre Dame Fighting Irish Football Team

*C*oach Knute Rockne's legendary "win one for the Gipper" speech inspired Notre Dame to a dramatic, come-from-behind victory against Army in 1928.

With the score 6–6 late in the fourth, Notre Dame's Butch Niemiec tossed one deep to six-foot-three Johnny O'Brien. The lanky receiver juggled the ball, corralled it, and dove into the end zone for the winning touchdown. Rockne was so moved that he ran to his heroic receiver and gave him a hug. The Irish fans screamed in delirium, unaware of what had inspired their men to such a tremendous upset.

But perhaps, high in the heavens, an inspiration named Gipp smiled with delight. He knew what had happened. The boys at Notre Dame had just won one for the Gipper.

The 132-foot-high mosaic of Christ can be seen in the background as a runner enters the tunnel to Notre Dame Stadium.

TEAM HISTORY

What though the odds be great or small,
Old Notre Dame will win over all.

O ver the years, those lines from the "Notre Dame Victory March" have held true for the Catholic university in South Bend, Indiana. Notre Dame teams have marched through a football schedule undefeated twenty-two times, most recently in 1988. Through the end of the twentieth century, their .753 winning percentage was the greatest of all time. When the Fighting Irish are down, they always seem to have a dramatic comeback in them.

A Winning Atmosphere

"Notre Dame is the easiest place in the world to win," said Lou Holtz, head coach of the 1988 national championship team. "The discipline and the love and the family atmosphere—and the intelligence and the commitment to excellence—all carry over onto the football field."[1]

Notre Dame is a relatively small university, with about ten thousand students. However, it is a close-knit community. The faculty and students pride themselves on academics and Christian values—as well as football. In fact, a symbol of the school is a 132-foot-high mosaic of Christ that overlooks Notre Dame Stadium. Because the arms of the image are raised, fans call him Touchdown Jesus. Since 1966, Notre Dame faithful have packed the stadium to capacity for every game but one. Through 2000, no school produced more Associated Press No. 1 rankings (eight) or fielded more Heisman Trophy winners (seven).

The Fighting Irish

The players on Notre Dame's first football team never dreamed it would turn out this way. On November 23, 1887, they invited the boys from Michigan to help teach them the game. That day, Notre Dame wound up losing a one-sided, 8–0 decision to the Wolverines. In December 1888, Notre Dame defeated Harvard Prep High School of Chicago, 20–0, for the first of their many victories. Through the 2000 season, only their "teachers" from Michigan could boast more wins in their history.

People still debate about how Notre Dame came to be called the Fighting Irish. Some say it began in 1899, with Notre Dame leading 5–0 at halftime of a game against Northwestern. Wildcats fans began chanting, "Kill the Fighting Irish! Kill the Fighting Irish!" Another

The Notre Dame Fighting Irish Football Team

story tells of a Notre Dame player yelling at his teammates during a 1909 game against Michigan: "What's the matter with you guys? You're all Irish and you're not fighting worth a lick."[2] The challenge prompted a come-from-behind victory for Notre Dame.

The nickname is most commonly attributed to the press. In the early days, sportswriters admired Notre Dame teams for their grit and determination—qualities that were associated with the Irish. The name stuck. And Notre Dame did, indeed, fight, fight, fight!

One of the first coaches, Jesse Harper, led the team to a 34–5–1 record over five seasons. The "glory days," though, started when a former player named Knute

Irish fans in Notre Dame Stadium cheer as Georgia Tech kicks off to Notre Dame on September 6, 1997.

Rockne took over the Irish in 1918. Rockne's second and third seasons featured the great George Gipp. In those seasons, the Irish hammered their opponents, going 9–0 both years. Three other Rockne-coached clubs also finished unbeaten and untied.

The Four Horsemen

Notre Dame's 1924 team featured the most famous backfield quartet in college football history. The names Harry Stuhldreher, Jim Crowley, Don Miller, and Elmer Layden might escape the memories of some, but who can forget the words of sportswriter Grantland Rice? "Outlined against a blue, gray October sky, the Four Horsemen rode again."[3]

The main secret to the success of the legendary backfield was the way they worked so well in combination with each other. Their timing on each play was almost always perfect. The Four Horsemen went on to lead the Irish to an undefeated season in 1924. The team's Rose Bowl victory over Stanford on January 1, 1925, earned Notre Dame its first undisputed national championship.

A Championship Tradition

Elmer Layden later coached the Irish, but it was under Frank Leahy in the 1940s that Notre Dame began its next dynasty. Though he coached for only eleven seasons, six of his teams were unbeaten. No one defeated Leahy's Irish for 39 games, from 1946 until the beginning of 1950.

*N*otre Dame's legendary Four Horsemen were, from left to right, Don Miller, Elmer Layden, Jim Crowley, and Harry Stuhldreher.

More than a decade passed without a national title before the Era of Ara brought Notre Dame back to the pinnacle in 1964. Ara Parseghian's 1966 and 1973 teams ruled college football, as did the 1977 Fighting Irish under Dan Devine. The 1977 champs featured a gritty, blond quarterback named Joe Montana, who represented Notre Dame's never-say-die spirit perhaps as well as anyone.

Another eleven-year national title drought followed before the magical Lou Holtz led the team back to greatness in 1988 with the school's first 12–0 season. And though more than a decade may pass without a final No. 1 ranking, legitimate title hopes are never far off under the golden dome.

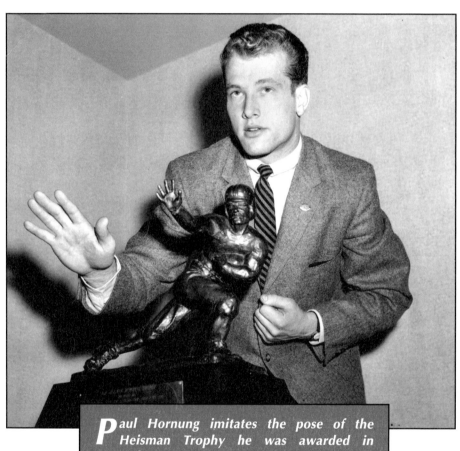

Paul Hornung imitates the pose of the Heisman Trophy he was awarded in December 1956. Hornung is the only player to win the Heisman while playing for a losing team.

THE LEGENDS

Notre Dame has fielded a record seven Heisman Trophy winners, including quarterbacks Angelo Bertelli (1943), Johnny Lujack (1947), Paul Hornung (1956), and John Huarte (1964). The other Heisman recipients were end Leon Hart (1949), halfback Johnny Lattner (1953), and flanker Tim Brown (1987). Featured here are the most legendary players in Irish history.

Johnny Lujack

Talk about a capable back-up! In the fall of 1943, quarterback Angelo Bertelli left for the marines. Johnny Lujack stepped in, beat Army, and helped complete a national championship season.

Lujack returned from a stint in the navy to direct undefeated teams in 1946 and 1947. By the start of his Heisman campaign of 1947, this national hero was receiving an average of three hundred fan letters per week.

A 1965 poll of sportswriters dubbed Lujack "the greatest Notre Dame back of the past 50 years."[1] Ironically, though he was known more for his skills on offense, the best play of his career may have been on defense. His touchdown-saving tackle of Doc Blanchard in 1946 preserved a scoreless tie with Army.

Leon Hart

Countless giants have roamed the line of scrimmage in South Bend. None have done it quite like Leon Hart, and perhaps none ever will.

Hart, starring in a day when playing both offense and defense was commonplace, stood out for several reasons, not the least of which was his character. On a 1947 team that many consider the greatest in college football history, Hart found a sign posted near the locker room. It gave a campus address for anyone interested in placing bets. Just a teenager in a room full of World War II vets, the muscular Hart ripped down the sign and shouted, "This has no place in a Notre Dame locker room!"[2]

Hart went on to command the respect of opponents, too. A blocking, pass-catching end who doubled as a nightmare on defense, Hart was voted Associated Press Male Athlete of the Year in 1949. At the end of the millennium, he was one of just two linemen ever to win the Heisman Trophy.

Paul Hornung

Dubbed the Golden Boy of Notre Dame, Paul Hornung remains the only player in history to win the Heisman on a losing team.

Hornung had been a multisport star at his Kentucky high school, and he turned down invitations from colleges all over the country. Before he even started a game, Coach Frank Leahy said, "Paul Hornung will be the greatest quarterback Notre Dame ever had."[3]

The fun-loving Hornung turned out to be a standout as a quarterback, halfback, fullback, safety, and kicker. The Irish were 2–8 in 1956, but in one game Hornung threw and ran for 354 yards—most in the nation that year. After the season, he accepted the bronze Heisman statue. Hornung went on to lead the NFL in scoring from 1959 to 1961, and won championships with the Green Bay Packers.

Joe Montana

Oh, could Joe Montana win a game—even before he became a Super Bowl MVP!

The quarterback of a national championship team in 1977, Montana saved his most memorable performance for the following season's Cotton Bowl. With ND trailing Houston, 34–12, Montana shook off an illness that sidelined him for the third quarter. He returned and went to work. After Steve Cichy returned a blocked punt for a touchdown, Montana ran for a score. He then found Kris Haines for an eight-yard TD pass as time expired that gave the Irish

*A*fter a brilliant college career at Notre Dame, quarterback Joe Montana went on to achieve even greater fame in the NFL. He was inducted into the Pro Football Hall of Fame in 2000.

a 35–34 win. "It beats every game we ever played," said Notre Dame athletic director Moose Krause.[4]

The "Comeback Kid" went on to win four Super Bowls. Many hail him as the greatest NFL quarterback of all time.

Tim Brown

From humble beginnings grew a Notre Dame star. Tim Brown fumbled a kickoff on the very first play of his very first season in blue and gold. Soon that 1984 miscue was long forgotten.

Brown's senior year started with a remarkable touchdown catch in double coverage that helped the Irish win at Michigan. In his next game, two breath-taking plays vaulted him to the front of the Heisman pack. In the home opener against Michigan State, Brown returned back-to-back punts for touchdowns of 71 and 66 yards.

By the time he left Notre Dame, Brown held nine-teen records as a receiver and return man. He went on to become one of the top wideouts in the NFL.

After setting nineteen school records at Notre Dame, Tim Brown joined the Oakland Raiders and became one of the best wide receivers in the NFL.

*N*otre Dame Coach Frank Leahy (right) chats
with University of Oklahoma Coach Bud
Wilkinson during a special dinner held by the
American Football Coaches Association in 1950.

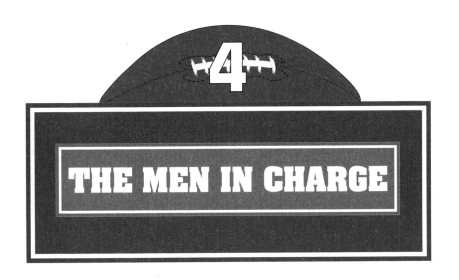

THE MEN IN CHARGE

Rockne and Leahy helped build the golden tradition of Notre Dame football in the first half of the twentieth century. Parseghian and Holtz helped revive it in the second half. The quartet combined to guide 11 national championship teams, and each man earned his place in Fighting Irish lore as a true coaching legend.

Knute Rockne

As a student at Notre Dame, Knute Rockne was a superior football player, a feared boxer, and an excellent student. He starred in stage plays, played the flute, and was one of the best marbles players on campus. After he became coach of the Irish in 1918, his innovative mind helped him become the most legendary college coach of all time.

In thirteen seasons, the Rock posted a 105–12–5 record. His .881 winning percentage remains the greatest ever. He ran the table, winning every game of a single season, five times.

Under Rockne, Notre Dame was the first team to play all over the country. His Irish shocked national powers, winning legions of fans as the victorious underdogs. Rockne designed his own equipment, making it lighter yet more protective. He also created the Notre Dame shift, in which all four backs changed positions before the ball was snapped.

After a championship season in 1930, Rockne died in a plane crash. Said columnist Will Rogers: "You died [as] one of our national heroes. Notre Dame was your address, but every gridiron in America was your home."[1]

Frank Leahy

Frank Leahy played tackle on Knute Rockne's last three Irish teams. His success rate as a Division I coach (.864, 107–13–9) stands second in Division I history behind Rockne's. Leahy coached at Notre Dame from 1941 to 1943 and 1946 to 1953—while serving in the navy in between. His teams of the late 1940s were among the mightiest in the history of college football.

Early in his Irish coaching career, some wondered whether Leahy was crazy for scrapping Rockne's offensive scheme. He employed a T-formation that he "borrowed" from Stanford and pro football's Chicago Bears. No one was arguing when his first team went 8–0–1 in 1941. His 1943 squad won the first of his four national titles.

A stickler for detail, Leahy once saw a violent rainstorm as an opportunity to have his team run an extra five laps in practice. He explained, "You never know what might happen on a Saturday."[2]

Ara Parseghian

The Era of Ara started with a basic principle: "Take the personnel, see what they can do best, and let them dictate strategy," Parseghian said. "Don't start with the strategy first."[3]

Few coaches in the history of football used their personnel as effectively as Parseghian. In his rookie season of 1964, he inherited a sub-.500 team and won nine of ten games. He was named National Coach of

Ara Parseghian instructs players on the College All-Stars team in 1976. Parseghian led Notre Dame to two national titles.

the Year. Two seasons later, Parseghian won the first of his two national championships (1966 and 1973).

Parseghian's teams included an army of rugged defensive stalwarts: Jim Lynch, Mike McCoy, Walt Patulski, Greg Marx, and Alan Page. Quarterbacks Terry Hanratty, Joe Theismann, and Tom Clements directed Ara's efficient attacks.

Lou Holtz

He was Notre Dame's little big man. "I'm five feet, ten inches and weigh 152 pounds," said Lou Holtz.

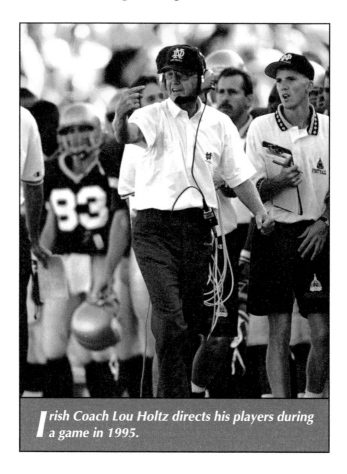

Irish Coach Lou Holtz directs his players during a game in 1995.

The Notre Dame Fighting Irish Football Team

"[I] speak with a lisp, appear afflicted with a combination of scurvy and beriberi, and I ranked 234th in a high school class of 278."[4] Yet, to Notre Dame fans, Holtz was nothing short of a savior for their football team.

Holtz was an offensive craftsman and a master motivator. He revived a floundering program and won a national championship in his third season. Though his first team, in 1986, matched the 5–6 record of the previous year, Irish fans could see a breakthrough on the horizon. It happened in a flash, as star receiver/return man Tim Brown dashed to the Heisman Trophy the following year. The 1988 team won all twelve of its games and a national title.

Several close calls followed. Holtz's 1989 and 1993 Irish teams each fell one win short of national championships, finishing No. 2 in the final AP poll.

Notre Dame Coach Knute Rockne addresses his team on September 15, 1930. The Irish went on to post a 10–0 season.

DREAM SEASONS

A t Notre Dame, some view a losing season as a year in which you lose just one game. Featured here are Irish teams that ran the table, winning every game in a single season.

1913

Try to imagine, for a moment, college football without the forward pass. Although it became a legal play in 1906, it was not until seven years later that it became popular. Notre Dame's 35–13 rout of mighty Army made the forward pass known as an effective way to move the ball.

Jesse Harper became Irish coach before the 1913 season. One of the first moves he made was to schedule a trip to West Point to strengthen the team's schedule. Army reluctantly agreed to pay Notre Dame $1,000 for its journey, feeling it would be a good investment for a victory. Gus Dorais had other ideas.

The Irish quarterback completed fourteen of seventeen passes for 243 yards, staggering totals for that era. It was the biggest triumph of the season for Notre Dame, which went 7–0.

1927-30

Knute Rockne delivered his famous "Win one for the Gipper" speech during this era of Irish football. However, it was Notre Dame's sustained excellence that made this four-year run one of the greatest ever.

The Irish went 7–1–1 in 1927 before beating Army in the famous "Gipp game" the following year. Then, in the last two years before Rockne's tragic death, his teams were unbeatable. The 1929 team won all nine games away from home, as Notre Dame Stadium was under construction. Green Bay Packers coach Curly Lambeau asked Rockne what kind of team he had for 1930. "It looks like the best I ever had," Rockne said. "But I'd never tell them that."[1] Quarterback Frank Carideo was the most prominent of seven All-Americans on that 10–0 juggernaut.

1946-49

There is a huge difference between college and professional football. Or is there? It all depends on whether your comparison includes Notre Dame's 1947 national championship team.

In an article entitled "The Year South Bend Had an NFL Franchise," Bill Furlong wrote: "There has never been a team with the . . . assurance that it could lose its

The Notre Dame Fighting Irish Football Team

first string, its second string, and perhaps even part of its third string, and still remain undefeated."[2]

Forty-two players from Notre Dame's 1947 squad played professional football. That number includes Heisman winners Johnny Lujack and Leon Hart. Notre Dame did not lose a game from the start of the 1946 season until October 7, 1950. Its 39-game unbeaten string featured a classic 0–0 tie with Army in 1946 and three national titles.

1966

On November 19, 1966, No. 1 Notre Dame and No. 2 Michigan State battled to the most famous tie in college football history. With their best offensive weapons, Nick Eddy and Terry Hanratty, out with

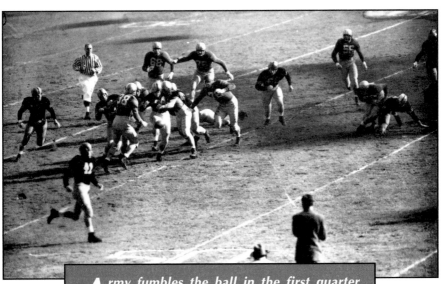

Army fumbles the ball in the first quarter against Notre Dame in their classic contest from 1946. The game ended in a scoreless tie.

injuries, the Irish rallied from a 10–0 deficit to tie the score, 10–10. Then, with the ball on their own 30-yard line and enough time for at least a few pass plays, Coach Ara Parseghian chose to run out the clock. "After [the comeback]," Parseghian said, "I didn't want to risk giving it to them cheap. They get reckless, and it could cost them the game."[3]

While some criticized the decision, it worked out well in the long run. Led by defensive All-Americans

Notre Dame Coach Lou Holtz is carried off the field by his players after the Irish beat West Virginia in the Fiesta Bowl on January 2, 1989. The victory capped a 12–0 season.

The Notre Dame Fighting Irish Football Team

Jim Lynch and Alan Page, Notre Dame (9–0–1) won its first consensus national title since 1949.

1988

Notre Dame's 1987 team lost its last three games and graduated Heisman Trophy winner Tim Brown. Many believed its young 1988 team was a year away from a title run. Lou Holtz told his players a different story. "I don't ever expect to lose another football game as long as I'm at Notre Dame," he instructed. "And I sure don't expect to lose one this year."[4]

What followed was the only 12–0 campaign in school history and Notre Dame's first national title since 1977. Quarterback Tony Rice and game-breaking receiver Raghib "Rocket" Ismail struck fear into opposing defensive coordinators. Defensive back Pat Terrell batted down a two-point conversion pass to preserve a 31–30 win over No. 1 Miami on the signature play of the year. The Irish capped the season with a 34–21 triumph over No. 3 West Virginia in the Fiesta Bowl.

*N*otre Dame Coach Bob Davie patrols the sidelines during a game against Stanford on October 7, 2000.

TODAY

Following Notre Dame's 1988 national championship, then-coach Lou Holtz reflected on coaching the Fighting Irish. "I had heard all the reasons it was difficult to win at Notre Dame—the high academic standards, the difficult schedule, the lack of an athletic dormitory," he said. "Notre Dame is no average school. Notre Dame is not comprised of average people. Notre Dame wants to be outstanding in all fields of endeavor."[1]

Fighting For Victories

Holtz's successor, Bob Davie, agrees that those same intangibles still exist at Notre Dame. Still, it's harder than ever to win in college football, as the level of competition intensifies every year. In 1999, the Fighting Irish crumbled under the pressure, winning five games and losing seven.

Quarterback Jarious Jackson was one of the lone bright spots in '99. The versatile senior broke Joe Theismann's single-season record for passing yardage. He also became the first player in Irish history to amass more than 3,000 yards in total offense in one year. Still, he couldn't help Notre Dame avoid its first seven-loss season since 1963.

"I realize we're supposed to win," Davie said after the season-ending loss to Stanford. "I realize we're not supposed to be 5-7. But you know something? There's a foundation being built."[2]

A Winning Season

Davie's remark turned prophetic. The fight of the Irish returned in the second game of the 2000 season. Notre Dame took No. 1 Nebraska to overtime before falling, 24-21. Proud Irish linebacker Rocky Boiman wasn't satisfied with just a moral victory. "We're Notre Dame," he said. "We played hard. We poured our hearts and souls into this game, and my guts are torn up inside."[3]

The next Saturday, the Irish beat a Rose Bowl-bound Purdue team, 23-21. Nick Setta boomed a 38-yard field goal as time expired. After a loss to Michigan State the next week, Davie installed a new quarterback, Matt LoVecchio. Led by this "one cool customer," as Davie called him, the Irish ripped off seven consecutive victories.

Notre Dame avenged its loss to Stanford, then knocked off Navy for the 37th straight time. After clubbing West Virginia, the Irish seemed on the brink

of losing to Air Force. However, Glenn Earl blocked a 28-yard field goal as time expired, and Notre Dame prevailed in overtime, 34-31. The Irish trounced Boston College and Rutgers, then climaxed the streak with a 38-21 whipping of rival Southern Cal.

On the season, LoVecchio tossed just one interception. The team committed just eight turnovers, tying an NCAA record. "We won . . . by doing it the old-fashioned way," said Davie, "with unselfish players, the kicking game, all those things."[4]

With a 9-2 record, and ranked 10th in the polls, ND earned a trip to the Fiesta Bowl. There they suffered a humbling loss to Oregon State, 41-9, as the Beavers out-hit and out-quicked the Irish.

An analysis of Notre Dame's 2000 season, as well as it 2001 recruiting class, indicates where Irish football is headed. Notre Dame lost out on the country's ultratalented recruits. However, the school did sign many quality student-athletes, kids whose lifelong dream was to play under the golden dome. It seems that in upcoming seasons the Irish will be a tough, gutty, opportunistic team, even if they won't have the talent to challenge for the national championship.

Davie, however, refuses to concede the ultimate victory. "We're farther along, in my opinion, than we've been since I've been head coach at Notre

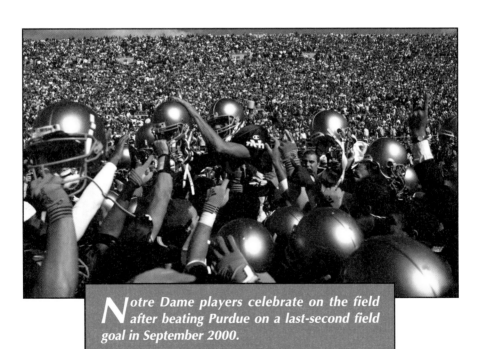

Notre Dame players celebrate on the field after beating Purdue on a last-second field goal in September 2000.

The Notre Dame Fighting Irish Football Team

Dame," he said. "The passion is there, the hunger is there."[5]

The Irish are still No. 1 when it comes to spirit and tradition. An early-1990s expansion of Notre Dame Stadium now has some 80,000 fans cramming into the "House that Rockne Built" for every Irish home game. Not only does ticket demand remain high, but so does national and international interest in ND football. NBC has televised all Irish home games over the past several years, and the broadcasts are seen as far off as Ireland, Japan, Panama, and Venezuela.

In a recent Harris Poll, Americans voted Michigan their third-favorite college football team. Florida State finished second. And the most beloved college team in the land? You guessed it: the winningest club in college football history. Notre Dame.[6]

STATISTICS

Team Record
Fighting Irish History

SEASONS	W	L	T	PCT.	BOWL RECORD	NATIONAL TITLES
1887–99	31	15	4	.660	–	None
1900–09	65	15	6	.791	–	None
1910–19	63	7	6	.868	–	None
1920–29	83	11	3	.871	1–0	1924, 1929
1930–39	66	20	5	.753	–	1930
1940–49	82	9	6	.876	–	1943, 1946, 1947, 1949
1950–59	64	31	4	.667	–	None
1960–69	62	34	4	.640	–	1966
1970–79	91	22	0	.805	6–2	1973, 1977
1980–89	76	39	2	.658	2–3	1988
1990–99	84	35	2	.702	4–5	None

The Fighting Irish Today

YEAR	W	L	T	PCT.	COACH	BOWL APPEARANCE	AP RANKING
1990	9	3	0	.750	Lou Holtz	Orange	6
1991	10	3	0	.769	Lou Holtz	Sugar	13
1992	10	1	1	.875	Lou Holtz	Cotton	4
1993	11	1	0	.917	Lou Holtz	Cotton	2
1994	6	5	1	.542	Lou Holtz	Fiesta	unranked
1995	9	3	0	.750	Lou Holtz	Orange	11
1996	8	3	0	.727	Lou Holtz	None	19
1997	7	6	0	.538	Bob Davie	Independence	unranked
1998	9	3	0	.750	Bob Davie	Gator	22
1999	5	7	0	.417	Bob Davie	None	unranked
2000	9	3	0	.750	Bob Davie	Fiesta	15

The Notre Dame Fighting Irish Football Team

Total History (through 2000)

W	L	T	PCT.	BOWL RECORD	NATIONAL TITLES
776	241	42	.753	13–11	11

W=Wins   L=Losses   T=Ties   PCT.=Percentage   AP=Associated Press

Coaching Records (since 1887)

COACHES	YEARS COACHED	RECORD	BOWL RECORD	NATIONAL TITLES
Morison, Hadden, Hering, McWeeny	1887–99	31–15–4	–	0
O'Dea, Faragher, Salmon, McGlew, Barry, Place, Longman	1900–10	69–16–7	–	0
Marks, Harper	1911–17	47–5–3	–	0
Rockne	1918–30	95–12–5	1–0	3
Anderson, Layden	1931–40	73–22–5	–	0
Leahy, McKeever, Devore*	1941–53	102–15–10	–	4
Brennan, Kuharich, Devore	1954–63	51–48–0	–	0
Parseghian	1964–74	95–17–4	2–2	2
Devine, Faust	1975–85	83–42–2	5–2	1
Holtz	1986–96	100–30–2	5–4	1
Davie**	1997–	30–19–0	0–3	0

*Ed McKeever and Hugh Devore coached during the 1944 and 1945 seasons while Frank Leahy was serving in the United States Navy.

**Stats through 2000

Great Fighting Irish Career Statistics

PASSING PLAYER	SEASONS	ATT	COMP	PCT.	YDS	TD
Angelo Bertelli	1941–43	318	167	.525	2,578	28
Johnny Lujack	1943; 1946–47	280	144	.514	2,080	19
Paul Hornung	1954–56	233	110	.472	1,696	12
John Huarte	1962–64	255	138	.541	2,543	17
Joe Theismann	1968–70	509	290	.569	4,411	31
Joe Montana	1975; 1977–78	515	268	.520	4,121	25

RUSHING PLAYER	SEASONS	ATT	YDS	AVG	TD
George Gipp	1917–20	369	2,341	6.3	21
Johnny Lattner	1951–53	350	1,724	4.9	20
Tony Rice	1987–89	384	1,921	4.9	23
Jerome Bettis	1990–92	337	1,912	5.7	27

RECEIVING PLAYER	SEASONS	REC	YDS	AVG	TD
Tom Gatewood	1969–71	157	2,283	14.5	19
Tim Brown	1984–87	137	2,493	18.2	12
Derrick Mayes	1992–95	129	2,512	19.4	22

PUNT RETURNING PLAYER	SEASONS	RETURNS	YDS	AVG	TD
Tim Brown	1984–87	36	476	13.2	3
Raghib Ismail	1988–90	25	336	13.4	1
Ricky Watters	1988–89	34	454	13.4	3

SEASONS=Seasons at Notre Dame
ATT=Attempts
COMP=Completions
PCT.=Percentage
YDS=Yards
TD=Touchdowns
AVG=Average
REC=Receptions
RETURNS=Punts returned

CHAPTER NOTES

Chapter 1. The Gipper

1. Gene Schoor, *100 Years of Notre Dame Football* (New York: William Morrow and Company, Inc., 1987), p. 44.

2. Ibid., p. 44.

3. Ibid., p. 38.

4. John U. Bacon, "This Is the Real Story of . . . The Gipper," *Detroit News Online*, January 7, 1997, <http://detnews.com/1997/college/9701/05/01050143.htm> (January 3, 2001).

5. Schoor, p. 57.

6. Ibid., p. 58.

Chapter 2. Team History

1. Lou Holtz with John Heisler, *The Fighting Spirit: A Championship Season at Notre Dame* (New York: Pocket Books, 1989), p. 379.

2. *1990 Notre Dame Football Media Guide* (South Bend, Ind.: University of Notre Dame, 1990), p. 338.

3. Grantland Rice, "The Four Horsemen," *Notre Dame Traditions*, n.d., <http://und.fansonly.com/trads/horse.html> (November 30, 2000).

Chapter 3. The Legends

1. Gene Schoor, *100 Years of Notre Dame Football* (New York: William Morrow and Company, Inc., 1987), p. 102.

2. Fred Katz, editor, *The Glory of Notre Dame* (Hong Kong: Bartholomew House Ltd., 1971), p. 77.

3. Ibid., p. 238.

4. Schoor, p. 209.

Chapter 4. The Men in Charge

1. Estate of Knute Rockne, "Knute Rockne Biography," *The Official Knute Rockne Web Site*, 2000, <http://www.cmgww.com/football/rockne/krbio.html> (July 26, 2000).

2. Fred Katz, editor, *The Glory of Notre Dame* (Hong Kong: Bartholomew House Ltd., 1971), pp. 74–75.

3. Tom Pagna with Bob Best, *Notre Dame's Era of Ara* (Huntsville, Ala.: The Strode Publishers, Inc., 1976), p. 36.

4. *1988 Notre Dame Football Media Guide* (South Bend, Ind.: University of Notre Dame, 1988), p. 104.

Chapter 5. Dream Seasons

1. Fred Katz, editor, *The Glory of Notre Dame* (Hong Kong: Bartholomew House Ltd., 1971), p. 53.

2. Ibid. p. 74.

3. *1990 Notre Dame Football Media Guide* (South Bend, Ind.: University of Notre Dame, 1990), p. 350.

4. Lou Holtz with John Heisler, *The Fighting Spirit: A Championship Season at Notre Dame* (New York: Pocket Books, 1989), p. 10.

Chapter 6. Today

1. Lou Holtz with John Heisler, *The Fighting Spirit: A Championship Season at Notre Dame* (New York: Pocket Books, 1989), p. 379.

2. Al Lesar, "Davie Keeps Flame of Optimism Burning," *South Bend Tribune*, November 29, 1999, p. B1.

3. "Irish Fall In Heartbreaker To No. 1 Nebraska," *Notre Dame Official Athletic Site*, 2000, <http://und.fansonly.com/sports/m-footbl/recaps/090900aaa.html> (Sept. 9, 2000).

4. "Davie Feels Comfort and Urgency," *Blue and Gold Illustrated*, 2001, <http://www.blueandgold.com/2001_march/lou_fb_0321.htm> (March 24, 2001).

5. Ibid.

6. Harris Poll of American Adults, *Notre Dame President's Newsletter*, October 1999.

GLOSSARY

All-American—Each season, numerous organizations announce a college football All-America Team. They select the best player at each position.

Associated Press poll—A poll of college football writers and broadcasters who vote on the nation's top twenty-five teams.

Cotton Bowl—Played in Dallas, traditionally on New Year's Day. From 1970 through 1994, Notre Dame played in seven of them, winning five.

end—A term most often used in prior eras, when players played both offense and defense. Comparable to today's tight ends and defensive ends.

Four Horseman—Notre Dame's great backfield quartet of Harry Stuhldreher, Jim Crowley, Don Miller, and Elmer Layden.

fullback—A powerful running back who lines up right behind the quarterback.

golden dome—The school's administration building is capped by a dome covered with gold leaf. It has become the symbol of the university.

halfback—A running back who's usually smaller than the fullback and lines up half as deep behind him.

Heisman Trophy—Presented to the top player in college football each season since 1936. Voted on by national media and former Heisman winners.

national championship—Previously, the team that finished No. 1 in the year-end polls—such as the Associated Press poll—was considered an unofficial national champion. Today, the No. 1 and 2 teams meet in a bowl game to decide a champion.

"Notre Dame Victory March"—The school's fight song, composed in 1908. It is now perhaps the most recognized fight song in America.

T-formation—When the fullback lines up directly behind the quarterback. Beside the fullback are the left and right halfbacks.

Touchdown Jesus—A 132-foot-high mosaic on the south side of Notre Dame's Hesburgh Library. The mural of Christ, hands raised, overlooks Notre Dame Stadium.

"Win one for the Gipper"—Against Army in 1928, the Irish strove to win the game for George Gipp, a great Notre Dame player who died during his senior season.

FURTHER READING

Chelland, Patrick. *One for the Gipper.* Loomis, Calif.: Arrowhead Classics, Inc., 1995.

Connor, Jack. *Leahy's Lads: The Story of the Famous Notre Dame Football Teams of the 1940s.* South Bend, Ind.: Diamond Communications, 1997.

Delsohn, Steve. *Talking Irish: The Oral History of Notre Dame Football.* New York: Avon Books, 1998.

Griffin, Gwen. *Irish Legends: The Notre Dame Fighting Irish Story.* Mankato, Minn.: The Creative Company, 1999.

Krause, Moose, and Stephen Singular. *Notre Dame's Greatest Coaches.* New York: Simon and Schuster, 1994.

Layden, Joe. *Notre Dame Football A–Z.* Dallas, Tex.: Taylor Publishing Company, 1997.

Marder, Keith, Mark Spellen, and Jim Donovan. *The Notre Dame Football Encyclopedia: The Ultimate Guide to America's Favorite College Football Team.* New York: Carol Publishing Group, 1999.

Pagna, Tom, and Bob Best. *Notre Dame's Era of Ara.* South Bend, Ind.: Diamond Communications, 1994.

Robinson, Raymond H. *Rockne of Notre Dame: The Making of a Football Legend.* New York: Oxford University Press, 1999.

INDEX

A
Air Force, 37
Army, 6, 8, 29, 31

B
Bertelli, Angelo, 17
Boston College, 37
Brown, Tim, 17, 20–21, 27, 33

C
Chicago Bears, 24
Cotton Bowl, 19
Crowley, Jim, 14–15

D
Davie, Bob, *34*, 35-38
Devine, Dan, 15
Dorais, Gus, 29

F
Fiesta Bowl, 33, 37
Florida State, 39
Four Horsemen, The, 14–15
Furlong, Bill, 30

G
Gipp, George, *4*, 5–9, 14
Green Bay Packers, 19, 30

H
Hanratty, Terry, 26, 31
Harper, Jesse, 13, 29
Hart, Leon, 17–18, 31
Harvard Prep High School, 12
Heisman Trophy, 12, *16*, 17–19, 27, 31, 33
Holtz, Lou, 11, 15, 23, 26–27, 32-33, 35
Hornung, Paul, *16*, 17, 19

H
Huarte, John, 17

I
Ismail, Raghib "Rocket," 33

J
Jackson, Jarious, 36, *37*

K
Krause, Moose, 20

L
Lambeau, Curly, 30
Lattner, Johnny, 17
Layden, Elmer, 14–15
Leahy, Frank, 14, 19, *22*, 23–25
LoVecchio, Matt, 36–37
Lujack, Johnny, 17-18, 31

M
Michigan State, 31
Michigan Wolverines, 12-13, 39
Miller, Don, 14-15
Montana, Joe, 15, 19, *20*

N
Navy, 36
Northwestern Wildcats, 12
Notre Dame Stadium, *10*, 12–13
Notre Dame Victory March, 11

O
Oregon State, 38

P
Page, Alan, 26, 33
Parseghian, Ara, 15, 23, 25, 32

R

Rice, Grantland, 14
Rice, Tony, 33
Rockne, Knute, 5–6, 8–9,
    13–14, 23–24, *27*, 30, 39
Rogers, Will, 24
Rose Bowl, 14, 36
Rutgers University, 37

S

Southern Cal, 37
Stanford, 14

Stuhldreher, Harry, 14–15
Super Bowl, 19

T

Theismann, Joe, 26, 36

W

West Virginia, 33, 36
Wilkinson, Bud, 22

Y

Yankee Stadium, 8

WHERE TO WRITE AND INTERNET SITES

University of Notre Dame
http://www.nd.edu/

Official Athletic Site of Notre Dame Fighting Irish Football
http://und.fansonly.com/sports/m-footbl/nd-m-footbl-body.html

Unofficial Home of Notre Dame
http://www.uhnd.com/

Irish Sports Report
http://irishsports.com/

Lets Go Irish!
http://www.letsgoirish.com/

The Official Web Site of George "The Gipper" Gipp
http://www.cmgww.com/football/gipp/index.html

The Official Knute Rockne Web Site
http://www.cmgww.com/football/rockne/index.html

University of
Notre Dame
Main Building #301
Notre Dame, IN 46556-5602

The Notre Dame Fighting Irish Football Team